START WITH WITH BISMILLAH

Ismail prudently waited for his mother to return home from work. She is a doctor at the city hospital. Once she got home, she rushed to Ismail's room to tell him a little story before bedtime.

Ismail used to love listening to his mother's stories. She would tell him Islamic stories every night, the missions of the prophets and their difficulties, and stories from the Quran. But this evening, Ismail looked worried. It was as if he had questions and was afraid to share them with his mother.

« Good evening my little Ismail, I hope you had a wonderful day at school. I'm sorry for being late tonight, my colleagues needed my help ».

« Ismail, my son, are you ready for tonight's story? » Mama told him with a big friendly smile. Ismail nodded and mom kissed him on his forehead. « This evening I will tell you the story of the great Prophet Mohamed S.A.W. », said Mama.

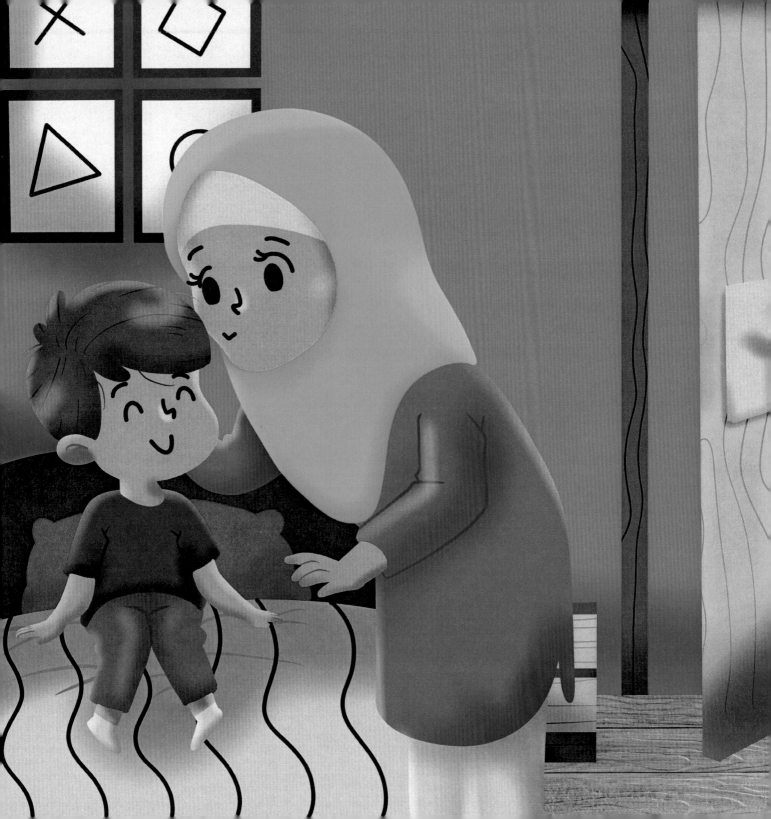

<< But mama!!! I have one more question >>, Ismail was interjecting with a frown. << Don't hesitate to ask any questions, my son >>. << Mom, can I fast tomorrow? >>, little Ismail asked innocently.

Mom laughed. << But you are still seven years old, Ismail >>, Mama replied, gently stroking his face.

<< But why do Muslims fast, Mama? >>, Ismail asked.

<< We fast because it is a duty to Allah (s.w.t.) >>, Mama replied. Ismail, however, was still far from satisfied with this answer.

My little Ismail! My son! Do you really believe that fasting only means not eating and drinking all day long?

Ismail answered in the affirmative with a nod of his head.

<< No, Ismail! My son! It is far more than that, fasting is also about our soul and spirit. We refrain from any sin during this holy month. We read the Quran every day and practice its teachings. We do as many good deeds as we can, and try to keep it a habit for the rest of the year. Ismail looked surprised. His eyes widened in amazement.

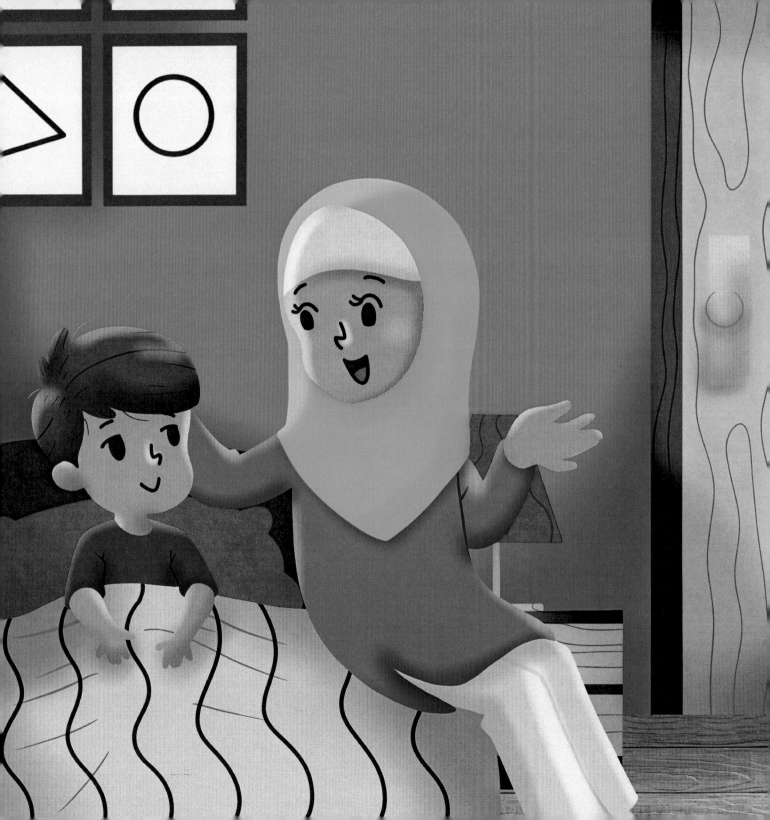

<< Mom, please let me fast tomorrow. I will recite the Holy Quran and behave as well as I can,>> Ismail pleaded with his mother. << But Ismail, Allah (s.w.t.) has not made it obligatory for you yet. You don't have to fast until you are older >>, the Ismail tried to convince

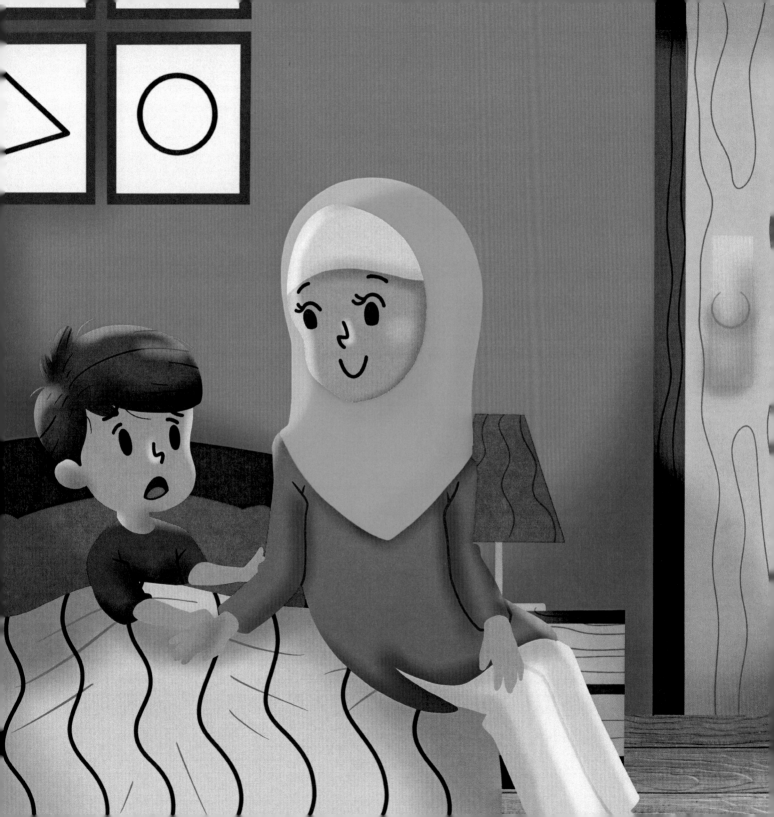

But Ismail was fascinated by the idea of fasting and kept asking his mother for permission.

<< Okay. Okay >>, mom finally said, raising her hands. << If you have the good intention (Niya) to fast, then I will allow you, but only on the condition that you stop if you are not well. May Allah accept your fasting >>.

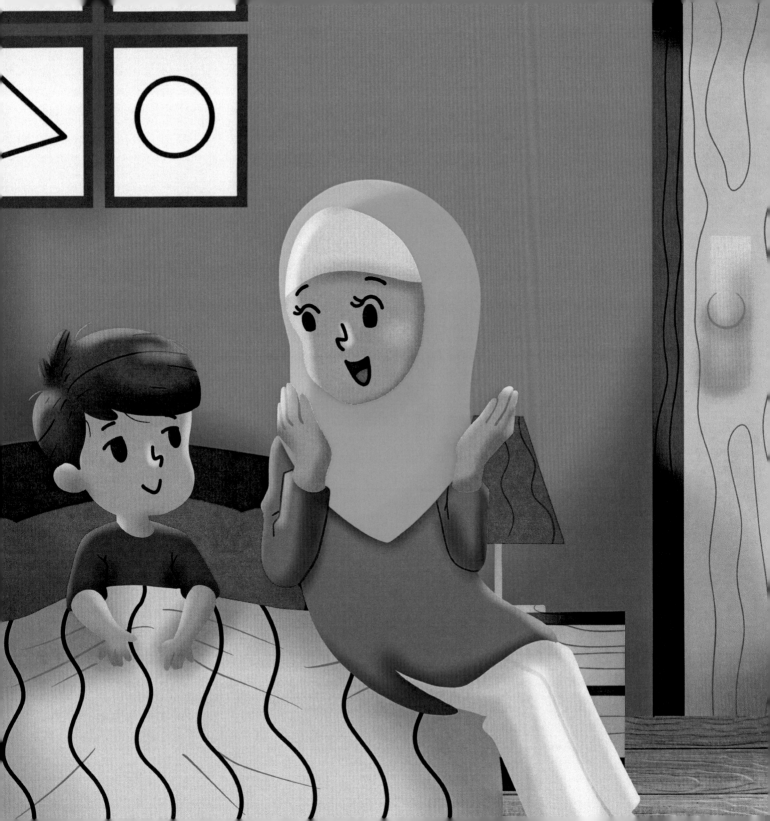

Ismail was jumping for joy. Mom put him to bed so he could wake up in time for breakfast before sunrise (Sahur). Ismail was so excited that he couldn't sleep. Mom would come into the room an hour before Fajr to wake Ismail up, but he was already awake.

He walked down the stairs and saw his father sitting at the dining table. His father gave him a smile.

<< Little Ismail is going to fast today, isn't he? >>, his father asked. Ismail excitedly nodded.

The little family ate their sahur in all spirituality. Dad was going to the mosque. Mom stayed at home and conducted her prayer and recited the Quran. After the Fajr prayer, they rested for a while.

Dad rose to go to work at the office. Ismail woke up and noticed that he was extremely hungry. He went to his mother who was preparing iftar (breaking of the fast) in the kitchen.

Ismail gazed excitedly at the beautiful marinated chicken.

The mother noticed Ismail and laughed.

<< What's going on, Ismail? Are you hungry already?>>, she asked with a smile.

<< No, mom. >> I'm not hungry at all<< Ismail didn't want to admit that he wanted to eat. >> Be careful, Ismail. << Allah prohibits us from lying during fasting<>, Mama replied.

<< Mom, this is harder than I thought >>, Ismail said in a sad voice.

<< Ismail, you are welcome to eat something if you want >>, mom replied worriedly. Ismail thought about it for a while. However, then he decided against it. He decided to read some verses from the Quran instead of watching TV.

As always, he performed his prayers on time. But the hunger became more and more unbearable. He thought about food all the time. He could relate to the feelings of those who did not have enough to eat in their daily lives. His empathy moved him to take a nap to rest.

Mom woke him up and informed him that it was only thirty minutes until iftar. He hurriedly hopped out of bed and hurried down the stairs. The table was already set, decorated with all of Ismail's favorite foods.

<< Tell me, Ismail. Have you fulfilled your duties as a good Muslim? >> his father asked politely.

<< Yes, Dad! I have avoided eating and drinking. Besides, I prayed on time, rendered the holy Quran, helped mom in the kitchen before lying down and thought about the good deeds I could do later >>.

Dad was looking very impressed. He held Ismail's little hands and kissed them lovingly.

<< Excellent, my son! Now lift your hands and thank Allah for His blessings and ask Him for mercy. Allah will accept all your prayers, inshallah.

The month of Ramadan is a month that tests our patience. All around us there is food, but we are not allowed to eat it. Ismail was making dua (supplication) with all his heart. Suddenly, the muezzin called the adhan. The mother gave Ismail a date to break his fast. Ismail felt happy as he ate his mother's food.

His heart was filled with contentment and gratitude.

He expressed his gratitude to Allah again for having food on the table and a place to sleep. Ismail pledged to remain a good Muslim throughout his life and to serve Allah Almighty (s.w.t.).

Thank you for purchasing our book

Your opinion is important to us

Made in United States
North Haven, CT
21 April 2022